WORLD RECORD BREAKERS

THE WORLD'S FASTEST MOTORCYCLES

BY ASHLEY P. WATSON NORRIS

Leslie Kendall, Curator
Petersen Automotive Museum,
Los Angeles, California

CAPSTONE PRESS
a capstone imprint

Edge Books are published by Capstone Press,
1710 Roe Crest Drive, North Mankato, Minnesota 56003
www.mycapstone.com

Library of Congress Cataloging-in-Publication Data
Library of Congress Cataloging-in-Publication data is available on the Library of
Congress Website
ISBN 978-1-4914-8178-3 (library binding)
ISBN 978-1-4914-8182-0 (paperback)
ISBN 978-1-4914-8186-8 (eBook PDF)

Editorial Credits
Mandy Robbins, editor; Sarah Bennett, designer; Morgan Walters, media researcher;
Laura Manthe, production specialist

Photo Credits
David Whealon, 11; Dreamstime: Typhoonski, 15; Getty Images: Heritage Images, 5;
Glow Images: Deposit Photos, 16-17; Mike Akatiff, 27, 28; Newscom: REBECCA COOK/
REUTERS, 22; Phil Hawkins, 20; Shutterstock: betto rodrigues, 18, Bykofoto, 19, Eky
Studio, design element, FotoYakov, design element, DEmax, design element, Mikael
Damkier, 7, Morphart Creation, top 9, Rainer Herhaus, cover, Seraphim Art, design
element, Wiktoria Pawlak, design element; Tara Bogart, 10; Wikimedia: cole24_, 24,
The Motorcycle Illustrated, bottom 9, Wendyhoney, 12

Printed in China.
007706

TABLE OF CONTENTS

SPEED IS KING!

Humans discovered the need for motorized speed in the late 1800s and early 1900s. This was an exciting time of invention, especially for vehicles. Animals were no longer needed to haul people from place to place. Motorcycles were invented around 1885. At that time they looked like bicycles with engines. But it didn't take long for engineers to begin pushing the limits of motorcycle speed and power.

The first motorcycle racers competed against automobiles at races in Europe. They were typically road races from town to town. In the United States, the first all-motorcycle race was held in Los Angeles, California, in 1901.

In the 1910s and 1920s, motorcycle races in the United States were held on wooden racetracks. These racing motorcycles were built for speed, not safety. They reached speeds up to 100 miles (161 kilometers) per hour and didn't have brakes. Wrecks were common and often deadly.

Motorcycle racer J.A. Watson-Bourne poses on a Brough motorcycle with company founder George Brough in the 1920s.

ENGINES

Over the years motorcycle racing has grown and changed. Strict safety rules keep riders and fans safe. There are divisions for different engine sizes, rider ages, and skill levels. One thing has remained the same, though—the desire to go fast.

Motorcycles use different types of engines. The various engines can be compared in a couple different measures. Cubic centimeters (cc) is a unit of volume showing how much air or liquid can be found in a cube that is 1 centimeter on every side. For vehicles, cubic centimeters measure how much volume is in the **cylinder**. The bigger the number, the more powerful the engine. Horsepower usually describes a car engine's power. It is sometimes also used when referring to an uncommonly powerful motorcycle. The more horsepower a vehicle has, the more power it has to push itself forward.

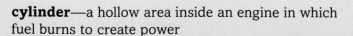

cylinder—a hollow area inside an engine in which fuel burns to create power

Motocross engines range in power from 50cc to 450cc.

CHAPTER 1
THE FIRST V-8 MOTORCYCLE

The world's first V-8 motorcycle was the Curtiss Custom V-8. A V-8 engine is one that has eight cylinders set in a "V" shape. Glenn Curtiss custom-built his V-8 engine for a **dirigible**. He later put the engine on a custom-made 8-foot- (2.4-meter-) long motorcycle frame.

The power from Curtiss' 40-horsepower engine went to the rear wheel. To stop, the rider shifted his weight onto a device on the back tire. At top speed it took the V-8 motorcycle 1 mile (1.6 km) to stop.

Curtiss wanted to find out how fast his motorcycle would go before giving it to the customer. On January 24, 1907, he set a speed record, blasting the V-8 motorcycle down the beach at 136.3 miles (219.4 km) per hour. The Curtiss V-8 motorcycle was not just the fastest motorcycle in the world in 1907. It was the fastest vehicle. No car, boat, motorcycle, or train had ever gone that fast.

dirigible—an aircraft that is powered by a motor and filled with a gas that makes it rise

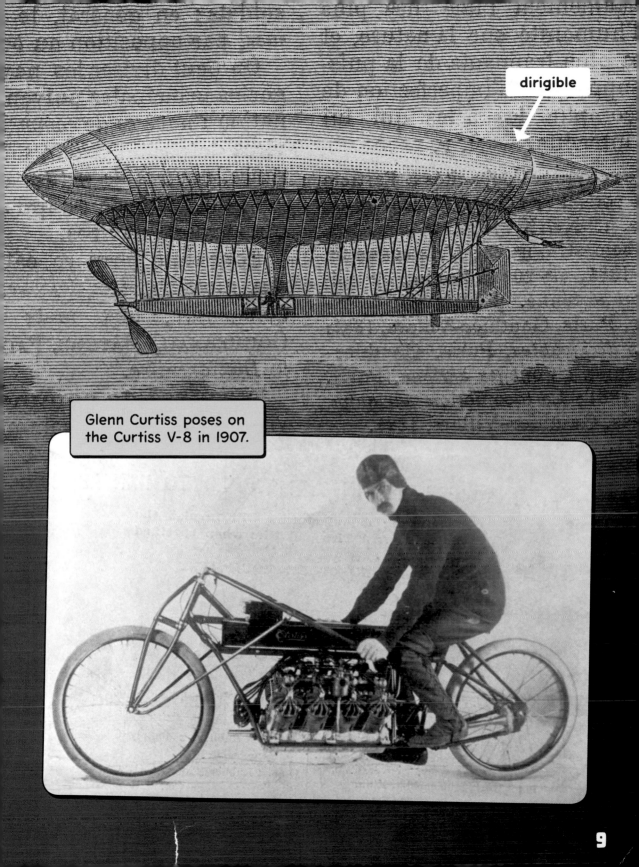

dirigible

Glenn Curtiss poses on the Curtiss V-8 in 1907.

CHAPTER 2

THE FASTEST DIRT BIKE

The Wolbrink Race KX500 is the world's fastest dirt bike. As a dirt bike, it can go off-road on rough **terrain**. After the race team modified it for land speed racing, Kevin Kilkenny set its fastest record of 131.418 miles (211.5 km) per hour in 2008.

Kevin Kilkenny (second from right) celebrates setting a speed record at the Bonneville Salt Flats with his team.

RACING LOCATIONS

Races for the title of fastest motorcycle in the world are held at many locations. The most famous is the Bonneville Salt Flats in Utah. It is 46 square miles (119 square km) of hard, flat, salt-covered land that is perfect for straight-line racing.

The Wolbrink Race team started with a **stock** Kawasaki KX500 dirt bike. They bought it for $5,000 and spent another $5,000 to fine-tune the performance of its engine. The stock KX500 is very tall. The rider has to stand on a bench and wear a heavy boot to kick-start the bike. In preparation for Kilkenny riding the bike, the team lowered the suspension. Smaller wheels, different gearing, and sleek bodywork were added to make the bike as fast as possible. At top speed, this KX500 can go only 5 miles (8 km) before it runs out of gas.

FACT

In 2009 Mark Wolbrink rode the stock KX500 to set the production dirt bike speed record at 125.85 miles (202.5 km) per hour. Rod Bush set the previous record of 123.75 miles (197.5 km) per hour back in 1981.

terrain—the surface of the land

stock—describes a motorcycle that has all of the parts that were installed at the factory

CHAPTER 3

THE FASTEST DIESEL MOTORCYCLE

The Crucible Die-Moto rocketed down the Bonneville Salt Flats at just over 130 miles (209 km) per hour in 2007. This feat made it the fastest diesel motorcycle in the world.

The Crucible Die-Moto runs on biodiesel instead of gasoline. The switch to biodiesel reduced the bike's pollution by 78 percent. Biodiesel is an environmentally friendly alternative to gasoline.

Crucible founder Michael Sturtz takes the Die-Moto for a test ride.

A group of artists, engineers, and motorcycle fans built the Die-Moto. They wanted to prove that motorcycles can be fast and environmentally friendly.

The Die-Moto is 9.8 feet (3 m) long and weighs 1,100 pounds (499 kilograms). This odd-looking motorcycle is pieced together from many different vehicles. It has a 163-horsepower BMW diesel car engine and two Honda car **radiators**. It also has BMW motorcycle **forks**, steering components, and wheels. The frame and all the other parts are custom-made.

The Die-Moto requires a lot of skill and concentration to ride. Engineers could not convert all the car pieces to work like a normal motorcycle should. The clutch for shifting gears uses a right foot pedal like a car instead of a lever on the right handlebar like a motorcycle. The rider leans forward on his chest to operate the bike and extends his right leg backward to shift gears. When the driver shifts, the bike can lean. At high speeds, this can be dangerous.

radiator—part of the vehicle through which the fluid flows so that it can be cooled

fork—the part of a motorcycle that connects the front wheel and axle to the bike frame

FACT

Riders wear a lot of gear to protect their bodies. Gear includes helmets, special boots, padded jackets, and pants.

CHAPTER 4

A SPEED LEADER IN PRODUCTION MOTORCYCLES

The Suzuki Hayabusa is among the fastest **production** motorcycles in the world. Stock models can reach 186 miles (299 km) per hour.

Hayabusa means "peregrine falcon" in Japanese. Suzuki channeled the power of this mighty bird in building its motorcycle of the same name. The bike has a 1,340-cc engine. Despite its amazing performance capabilities, the Hayabusa is accessible to the public. It costs about $15,000 and is mass-produced.

A highly customized Hayabusa set a record of 311.945 miles (502 km) per hour in 2011 at Loring Air Force Base in Maine. This bike had a turbocharger and custom **aerodynamic fairings**. Its speed made it the fastest open-cockpit motorcycle ever timed.

production—describes a vehicle manufactured for mass-market sale

aerodynamic—the ability of something to move easily and quickly through the air

fairings—the outer coverings of a motorcycle that helps the bike cut through the air

In 2000 motorcycle makers agreed to limit speed in production motorcycles. Most of today's mass-produced, road-worthy bikes are limited to a top speed of 186 miles (299 km) per hour.

TIMING MOTORCYCLE SPEED

A precise process is used to time motorcycle speed during a land speed race. In land speed racing one motorcycle travels in a straight line to set a speed record. Electronic equipment sends a beam of light across the racetrack to a receiver. When a motorcycle breaks the light beam, its speed can be calculated.

The Hayabusa is a street-legal motorcycle.

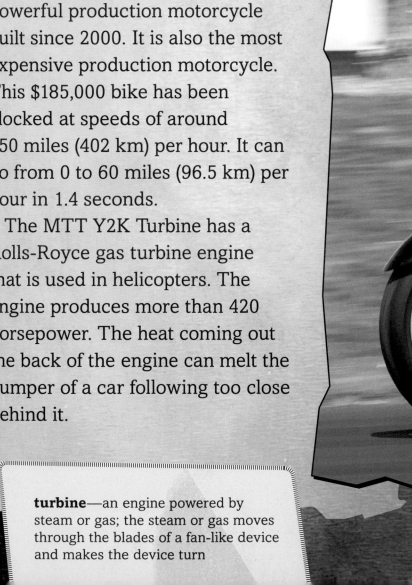

CHAPTER 5

FAST AND EXPENSIVE

The MTT Y2K **Turbine** Superbike holds two Guinness World Records. It is the most powerful production motorcycle built since 2000. It is also the most expensive production motorcycle. This $185,000 bike has been clocked at speeds of around 250 miles (402 km) per hour. It can go from 0 to 60 miles (96.5 km) per hour in 1.4 seconds.

The MTT Y2K Turbine has a Rolls-Royce gas turbine engine that is used in helicopters. The engine produces more than 420 horsepower. The heat coming out the back of the engine can melt the bumper of a car following too close behind it.

turbine—an engine powered by steam or gas; the steam or gas moves through the blades of a fan-like device and makes the device turn

FACT

Marine Turbine Technologies produces only four or five Y2Ks per year.

CHAPTER 6
FASTEST PRODUCTION TRACK MOTORCYCLE

New to the market, the 2015 Kawasaki Ninja H2 may reach speeds of 280 miles (451 km) per hour. It has a 998-cc engine with a supercharger. The bike is priced at $30,000. Only a limited number will be sold each year.

Wind tunnel testing was used to create the aerodynamic body design of the Ninja H2. Wings on the front create **downforce**. They keep the bike from lifting off the ground at high speeds.

This motorcycle is meant to be driven on the racetrack only and comes with racing slick tires. It does not have rearview mirrors, turn signals, or other parts needed for street-legal bikes. Buyers of a Ninja H2 have to sign a form agreeing not to drive it on public roads.

2015 Kawasaki Ninja H2

FACT

The Ninja H2 is loud. Noise is measured in **decibels**, and the Ninja H2 measures 120 decibels. That's as loud as a rock concert or ambulance siren. It can cause permanent hearing loss.

Racers lean into a curve during a 2015 Moto Grand Prix race in Spain.

MOTORCYCLE RACING

Many different types of motorcycle races exist, including motocross, endurance, road races, and ice races. Different types of bikes are designed for each type of racing. Moto Grand Prix is an 18-race series with multiple **superbikes**, such as the Ninja H2, racing around a track at the same time.

downforce—the force of passing air pressing down on a moving vehicle

decibel—a unit for measuring the volume of sounds

superbike—a high-performance motorcycle with a large engine, usually between 800 and 1,200-cc

19

CHAPTER 7

THE FASTEST ELECTRIC MOTORCYCLE

The KillaJoule is the world's fastest electric motorcycle. It also holds the record for the world's fastest sidecar motorcycle. Its official speed record is 240 miles (386 km) per hour. Its top speed so far is 270 miles (434.5 km) per hour.

Electric motorcycles and cars are becoming more common every day. They are important because they are better for the environment. A standard combustion engine burns gasoline. An electric vehicle runs on batteries that are rechargeable. They are recharged by special high-voltage electric cords. It usually takes a few hours to recharge a vehicle.

The KillaJoule blasts down Utah's Salt Flats in 2012.

The KillaJoule is a completely enclosed motorcycle called a streamliner. It is shaped like a teardrop or bullet. It is designed to move through the air as quickly as possible. The fairing covers the entire motorcycle, including the wheels and rider. The KillaJoule runs on 224 battery cells. Together these cells weigh 300 pounds (136 kg). These same batteries are used in electric cars. The KillaJoule's batteries cost $15,000.

The KillaJoule is 19 feet (5.8 meters) long and weighs 1,540 pounds (698.5 kg). It took a year to build. The battery cells produce power equal to 400 horsepower.

After every run, the batteries take two hours to recharge. During a land speed race, the team switches out the batteries for fresh ones for the second timed run.

The owner, designer, and pilot of this bullet was Eva Hakansson. The KillaJoule's world record of 270 miles (434.5 km) per hour makes Hakansson the fastest woman on a motorcycle!

FACT

Riders of streamlined vehicles, such as the KillaJoule, are also called pilots or drivers. "Pilots" is used because these vehicles go fast like a jet. "Drivers" is used because people sit in the motorcycle instead of riding on it. All three terms are correct.

CHAPTER 8

TOO FAST TO RIDE

The builders of the Dodge Tomahawk describe it as a sculpture that can be ridden. This bike is not street-legal. It weighs 1,500 pounds (680 kg). That's two to three times the weight of most **cruiser**-style motorcycles. The Tomahawk has two front tires and two back tires. They help the motorcycle remain stable and get enough traction to speed up. It has headlights located between the front wheels.

Dodge introduced the Tomahawk at a Detroit auto show in 2003.

cruiser—a style of motorcycle where the rider is slightly reclined

This beast of a motorcycle has a Dodge Viper car engine. The engine can propel the bike to speeds estimated at 300 to 350 miles (483 to 563 km) per hour.

The rider sits on top of the bike, unprotected from the wind. Its top speed has not been tested because the machine would be unsafe for the rider. At around 200 miles (322 km) per hour the wind would actually lift the rider up out of the seat.

The V-10 Viper engine pumps out an astounding 500 horsepower. It can push the Tomahawk from 0 to 60 miles (97 km) per hour in 2.5 seconds!

STRAIGHT OUT OF THE MOVIES

Two Dodge employees asked their bosses for permission to build a motorcycle with a Viper V-10 engine. Their vision was inspired by the four-wheeled motorcycle shown in the 1982 movie *Tron*. From concept to completion it took their team eight months to build the first Dodge Tomahawk.

FACT

The Dodge Tomahawk costs $550,000. Only nine have ever been built.

CHAPTER 9

STREAMLINED SPEED

The Bub 7 has set several world records. In 2006 it set a land speed record at just over 350 miles (563 km) per hour. That record was broken in 2008. But in 2009 the Bub 7 reclaimed the world land speed record at 367 miles (591 km) per hour. Its top recorded speed during the race was 372 miles (599 km) per hour.

The Bub 7 looks more like a missile than a motorcycle.

The Bub 7 streamliner was designed for one purpose—to break the land speed record. It pumps out 500 horsepower through its turbocharged 3,000-cc engine. The pilot, Chris Carr, covered 1 mile (1.6 km) in less than 10 seconds! Designed and built from scratch, it is an engineering marvel. The steering controls are the same ones found in an F-4 Phantom fighter jet. The clutch is from an Indy race car.

The Bub 7 runs on methanol, a fuel used in some race cars. Methanol lights on fire at a higher temperature than gasoline. A methanol fire can also be extinguished with water. That is important for pilot and team safety.

RECORD CHASERS

A lot of time, effort, and money go into the design and building of a high-speed motorcycle meant to break world speed records. The owners, team members, and pilots chase the dream of holding a land speed record. A land speed record cannot be owned. It is only borrowed until the next speed-demon comes along to challenge the title.

CHAPTER 10

THE FASTEST OF THE FAST

The Ack Attack is the fastest motorcycle in the world. It set the world record of 376 miles (605 km) per hour at the Bonneville Salt Flats in 2010. Its official top speed is 394 miles (634 km) per hour. Unofficially it can pass 400 miles (644 km) per hour.

The Ack Attack motorcycle is a streamliner more than 19 feet (5.8 m) long. It has two 1,300-cc Suzuki Hayabusa engines with turbochargers and 35 pounds (16 kg) of boost. These modifications help the engine reach 1,000 horsepower.

The Ack Attack uses 118-octane gasoline, which is also used in most types of motorsports racing engines. It guzzles 4.1 gallons (15.5 liters) of gas during an 11-mile (18-km) run. Its two racing tires are designed for speeds of more than 500 miles (805 km) per hour. The Ack Attack has two chains that combine the power of the two engines.

To stop the Ack Attack, the pilot squeezes the right hand brake lever to release a parachute. Even with the parachute it takes 5 miles (8 km) to fully stop the Ack Attack.

The Ack Attack looked like a giant blue bullet blasting down the Bonneville Salt Flats.

The Ack Attack is faster than a Ferrari, Lamborghini, or Porsche sports car.

Rocky Robinson has been the pilot for all three of the Ack Attack's record-setting runs. In 2006 he set a world record on Ack Attack traveling just under 343 miles (552 km) per hour. In 2008 he beat his previous world record by going 360.913 miles (580.8 km) per hour. Robinson's 2010 run holds the world record at 376 miles (605 km) per hour. He is one of the four people in the world qualified to drive a streamline motorcycle. Every time Robinson drives, he always carries a different good luck charm in his pocket.

With high speed comes danger, and the Ack Attack has been in three serious crashes. In the biggest crash it was going faster than 300 miles (483 km) per hour. It rolled 16 times, but Robinson walked away without serious injuries.

Pilot safety is a priority. The pilot is strapped into the bike with a nine-point safety harness. Arm and leg restraints are locked into the safety harness. During a crash, the harness and restraints keep the pilot's entire body safely inside the motorcycle. The bike has two fire prevention systems. The pilot wears a **fire-retardant** racing suit, gloves, boots, and head sock. The helmet has a fire-retardant lining.

The Ack Attack may currently hold the title of the world's fastest motorcycle, but it won't forever. If one thing is certain, it's that humans love nothing more than pushing limits, and the limits of speed are no exception. Only time will tell how fast the motorcycles of the future will go.

Rocky Robinson (center in ball cap) poses with his team next to the Ack Attack.

fire-retardant—a chemical that prevents a fire from spreading

GLOSSARY

aerodynamic (air-oh-dye-NAM-ik)—built to move quickly through the air

cruiser (KROO-zuhr)—a style of motorcycle where the rider is sitting upright or slightly reclined

cylinder (SI-luhn-duhr)—a hollow area inside an engine in which fuel burns to create power

decibel (DE-suh-buhl)—a unit for measuring the volume of sounds

dirigible (DEER-uh-juh-buhl)—an aircraft that is filled with a gas that makes it rise and powered by a motor

downforce (DOUN-fors)—the force of passing air pressing down on a moving vehicle

fairings (FAYR-ingz)—the outer coverings of a motorcycle that helps the bike cut through air

fire-retardant (FYRE ri-TAR-dent)—a chemical that prevents a fire from spreading

fork (FORK)—the part of a motorcycle that connects the front wheel and axle to the bike frame

production (pruh-DUHK-shuhn)—describes a vehicle manufactured for mass-market sale

radiator (RAY-dee-ay-tuhr)—part of the vehicle through which the fluid flows so that it can be cooled

restraint (rih-STRAYNT)—something that holds someone back

stock (STOK)—describes a motorcycle that has all of the parts that were installed at the factory

superbike (SOO-per-byke)—a high-performance motorcycle with a large engine, usually between 800 and 1,200-cc

terrain (tuh-RAYN)—the surface of the land

turbine (TUR-bine)—an engine powered by steam or gas; the steam or gas moves through the blades of a fanlike device and makes it turn

READ MORE

Aloian, Molly. *Motorcycles.* Vehicles on the Move. New York: Crabtree Pub., 2011.

Enz, Tammy. *Batmobiles and Batcycles: the Engineering Behind Batman's Vehicles.* Batman Science. North Mankato, Minn.: Capstone Press, 2014.

Lüsted, Marcia Amidon. *The Science of Motorcycle Racing.* The Science of Speed. North Mankato, Minn.: Capstone Press, 2014.

INTERNET SITES

FactHound offers a safe, fun way to find Internet sites related to this book. All of the sites on FactHound have been researched by our staff.

Here's all you do:

Visit www.facthound.com

Type in this code: 9781491481783

Check out projects, games and lots more at
www.capstonekids.com

CRITICAL THINKING
FOR THE COMMON CORE

1. Why do you think that the world's fastest motorcycles are not usually sold to the public? (Integration of Knowledge and Ideas)

2. Loring Air Force Base in Maine and the Bonneville Salt Flats in Utah are both places where speed records have been set. What type of land features do you think are ideal when it comes to chasing land speed records? (Key Ideas and Details)

INDEX